For Kyle Pirotta – S.G.
For all the staff and pupils at Chapel Allerton Primary School – S.A.

Text copyright © 2002 Sam Godwin
Illustrations copyright © 2002 Simone Abel
Volume copyright © 2002 Hodder Wayland

Series concept and design: Liz Black
Book design: Jane Hawkins
Commissioning Editor: Lisa Edwards
Editor: Katie Orchard
Science Consultant: Dr Carol Ballard

Published in Great Britain in 2002 by Hodder Wayland,
an imprint of Hodder Children's Books

Cataloguing in publication data
  Godwin, Sam
    Which Switch is Which?: A first look at electricity (Little Bees)
      1. Electricity - Juvenile literature
      I. Title
      537

    ISBN 0 7502 3801 1

    Printed and bound in Grafiasa, Porto, Portugal

    Hodder Children's Books
    A division of Hodder Headline Limited
    338 Euston Road, London NW1 3BH

Which Switch is Which?
A first look at electricity

Which Switch is Which?
A first look at electricity

Sam Godwin

HODDER
Wayland

an imprint of Hodder Children's Books

It is night-time. All is quiet and still.

Come on, let's find something to eat.

7

It is difficult to see in the dark.

9

So we turn on the lights.

I'll turn on this switch – three cheers for electricity!

11

Electricity comes from a power station.

It flows along wires and into our homes.

So, the wires must come in through a hole in the wall!

13

Other wires carry the electricity around the home,

Mummy, where are the wires for this switch?

Sometimes, wires are hidden inside a wall.

14

to switches in every room.

That's neat and tidy!

And more wires carry the electricity

That silly moth keeps flying towards the light.

from the switches to the lights.

17

Electricity not only gives us light.

20

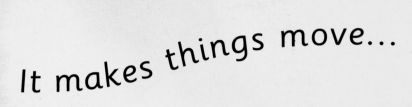

It makes things move...

What's this, Mummy?

It's a plug. Plugs connect things to the switches.

This washing machine uses electricity, too.

22

23

26

... and it can make things hot.

Let's see what this one does...

All about electricity

When it's dark, we need electric light to be able to see clearly.

Electricity travels into our homes along wires. The wires are connected to switches around the home.

Pressing a switch turns a light on.

Pressing a switch turns a light off.

Electricity makes lots of things work around the home.

It can make things hot or cold.

It can make sound.

And it can make things move.

Useful Words

Plug
This connects electrical objects to switches.

Power station
A place where electricity is made.

Shock
Electricity can pass through people and give them a nasty shock.

Switch
This can turn on or off the supply of electricity to an object.

Important
Electricity can be dangerous:
- Always ask an adult to turn on switches for you.
- Never touch any switches or plugs with wet hands.
- Never play with electric objects.